BEAM LIFE

THE LIFE JOURNAL

HOW TO GET UNSTUCK AND BE EVERYTHING AND MORE IN 90 DAYS

KAITLIN ANTHONY

ISBN: 979-8-218-09752-3 (paperback)

ISBN: 979-8-218-10131-2 (hardcover)

DISCLAIMER

The information contained in this journal is for informational purposes only. No material in here is intended to be a substitute for professional medical advice, diagnosis or treatment. Always seek the advice of your physician or other qualified health care provider with any questions you may have regarding a medical condition or treatment and before undertaking a new health care regimen, and never disregard professional medical advice or delay in seeking it because of something you read in this journal.

INTRODUCTION: A MESSAGE FROM YOUR COACH

The fact that you're reading this means you're probably *tired of feeling stuck and stressed*, but you don't know where or how to start changing that. Like so many people feeling the same way, it probably feels overwhelming to choose yourself and your goals.

You may be feeling a little gun-shy when it comes to investing in yourself, either because it's new territory for you or you've tried to get help before and it didn't work out the way you hoped it would—or perhaps advocating for yourself felt *completely unnatural and icky* because you've become so used to *putting everybody else in your life first,* before your own needs, desires, dreams and goals.

Any time you've tried to reclaim some "me time" or take your power back, you've probably experienced that *sinking, gut-wrenching feeling*—like the time you bought that fabulous luxury white couch only to be left with *buyer's remorse* after your kids stained it in under five minutes.

In the past when you tried to invest in your future, maybe you felt shaken together like an expert cocktail with a heavy pour of panic, imposter syndrome, and maybe a dash of mom guilt mixed in for good measure. Or when the time to perform came, your stomach churned, and your nerves got the best of you.

You know the feeling—the one where you have the big, exciting emotional build-up of *finally doing something for yourself…* that ultimately leads to the crash-and-burn of a major letdown that implodes your insides.

Ugh. It's less like a refreshing mocktail and more of a heady concoction that leaves you with an emotional hangover...but if you can relate, then this is *exactly* why I decided to create this journal for you.

After surviving an ugly divorce, becoming a mom, making three major career transitions, losing 100 pounds, and coming out as queer at 33, I have come out on the other side. Today, I'm proud to have competed in major physical endurance events and embraced entrepreneurship—and after 10 years of coaching women, I know a thing or two about self-belief and goalisetting.

I wanted you to be able to have the access and ability to live your Happily Ever *Now*, without feeling like you need to invest heavily in a coach or a program.

Because I'm such a believer in women building up other women and the possibilities that come from spending quality time with yourself, in this journal, I'm sharing with you the proven framework I use to help my clients achieve life-changing transformations in just 90 days.

Over the next 90 days, you will grow and become more confident in the areas of:

- Effective goal-setting
- Gratitude
- Tracking progress
- Celebrating wins
- Self-care
- Setting boundaries
- Confronting limiting beliefs

And more.

BEAM stands for Be Everything And More, which is what I believe is possible for you if you make this journaling practice a consistent part of your life.

I want you to know that *you're not alone* in where you are right now. How you feel is totally normal for so many women—*but it doesn't have to be your normal anymore!*

GETTING STARTED

How many times have you thought to yourself, *I wish I could*:

-Just lose 15 pounds
-Quit my job and start a business
-Spend more time with my kids
-Travel more
-Get out of debt
-Stress less

I'm going to let you in on a secret as to why you haven't achieved these things (yet)—and it's not your fault! Most of us have never been taught how to actually set effective goals, create accountability, or move the needle. Well, those days are over. With that out of the way, are you ready?

The secret is this: achieving goals takes clarity, accountability, action, a plan, belief, and consistency—NOT PERFECTION.

I'm not only going to tell you how to create a plan, but I'm going to take your hand and walk with you arm-in-arm for the next 90 days. Although this journal is only set up for 90 days, I recommend keeping this practice up for as long as you can, since your goals and desires will continue to grow and evolve with you.

The BEAM Life Journal is divided up into five parts:

Part I: Clarify Your Goal and Manifest Your Desires

Part II: Focus Your Attention on Creating Your Dream Life by Using SMAART Goals

Part III: Strategize Your Goals Over 90 Days

Part IV: Daily Journal Prompts for Progress Tracking, Gratitude, and Taking Action

Part V: Celebrate

To get the most out of this journal, I suggest you complete Parts I-III before moving on to the daily journal section in Part IV.

I can't wait to hear about your breakthroughs and discoveries; they are truly what I *live for*!

Be sure to scan this QR code to join the *free* BEAM Life: Build Your Dream Life community on Facebook, where you can connect with other like-minded women ready to reclaim their sense of self and *show up* fearlessly!

PART I: CLARIFY

Before you go further, know that this is the *most important part* of the journal! The rest of what follows is built off the clarity you gain from this section, as a lack of clarity and direction are the main reasons why most women feel stuck and frustrated with their current state of life (and I'm guessing it's why you do, too).

Nowadays, most of us can't get to the local Starbucks without GPS, so why is it when it comes to setting goals, we completely skip over being clear about where we want to take our lives? Sounds pretty logical when you think about it that way, huh?

Still, it's not your fault; you've probably never been taught how to properly manifest your dream life or set an effective goal. Well babe, those days are over!

I'm about to ask you 11 thought-provoking questions that, if taken seriously, will provide clarity on what you really want for yourself and your life. It's with this newfound clarity that we will be able to create effective goals and then, most importantly, take action.

For best manifesting practices, I advise the following:

- Set aside dedicated time to work through these questions, which also means notifying anyone else in your household not to disturb you.
- Pick an environment that sparks creativity and makes you feel comfortable.
- Turn off all your phone notifications—or better yet, leave your phone behind entirely! You don't need it.
- Avoid entering your sacred time hungry, sick, angry, tired, tipsy or in any other negative, mind-altered state.
- If you get stuck, take a break. You don't need to do everything in one day. Remember: there are no unrealistic expectations here!
- Feeling emotional is completely normal! More likely than not, this will be the first time you're admitting to yourself what you really want and need.
- Do a breathing or meditation practice before starting so you can gain focus and set an intention.
- Check in throughout the process and make sure you're manifesting and getting clarity on a life *you* really want, not the life someone else wants for you.
- LET GO of any perfectionist tendencies and judgments and allow your mind and pen to *flow*. You

can think about what you write later; right now, it's about getting it out of you.

Okay, the time has come to get you some clarity.

Let's get manifesting, babe!

Answer the following questions to help you get crystal clear on your biggest desires.

1. What's currently working and not working in your life right now? It can help to make a list of all the routines and habits that make you feel good as well as things you hold onto, feel responsible for, take up your time and energy or bring you stress.

_____

_____

_____

_____

_____

_____

_____

2. What are you committed to having in your life right now? Think life, but also specifically health, career, relationships, wellbeing, finances, etc.

_____

_____

_____

_____

_____

3. What's *really* keeping you from having these things?

_____

_____

_____

_____

_____

4. If you were able to move all the circumstances you listed in question three out of the way, what would be possible for you? What are you ready to let go of so you can step into this life?

_____

_____

_____

_____

_____

_____

_____

_____

_____

5. What can you do the next time one of these limiting beliefs or circumstances arises?

_____

_____

_____

_____

_____

6. What are the special and unique gifts that you bring to the world?

_____

_____

_____

_____

_____

_____

7. Visualize the best version of yourself that you can think of. What 3-5 words describe that version of you? How do you spend your time? How do you move throughout your day? How do you take care of yourself?

_____

_____

_____

_____

_____

_____

8. How do you want to feel every day? What experiences or habits support that? Write a timeline for the most fulfilling and happy day you could possibly have.

_____

_____

_____

_____

_____

_____

9. What truly lights you up and makes you BEAM? What can't you get enough of?

_____

_____

_____

_____

_____

_____

_____

10. What would it look like to live the life you deserve and desire?

_____

_____

_____

_____

_____

_____

_____

11. What are three things you can either add, change, remove, or make better in the next 90 days that will move the needle closer to the life you just manifested?

_____

_____

_____

_____

_____

_____

_____

Congrats, babe! You just completed a life-changing exercise that will surely accelerate the changes you've been dreaming of!

Support, accountability, and connection with other like-minded women is the secret sauce to making this manifestation come to fruition! Be sure to join the private Build Your Dream Life Facebook group using the QR code below and share your discoveries.

PART II: FOCUS

This is the part where we work together to make all those dreams you just manifested into a reality. I mentioned to you that most women are stuck because they lack clarity, but when you combine that with ineffective goal-setting, it's a literal dumpster fire. I often say, "A dream without a plan is just a dream."

The first time I saw the magic of creating and following a plan was when I trained for my first full marathon in 2011. I had little to no running experience and had just lost 80 pounds over the previous year and a half. Along with the guidance of a trainer and a few books, I created my first training plan. That little plan got me confidently from the couch to being able to run 26.2 miles through a monsoon. If you happened to run the LA Marathon in 2011, you know exactly what I mean —but I digress.

Creating and following that training plan—key word being "following"—truly changed my life. I experienced first-hand how small daily actions can compound to get you across the finish line, literally.

From that moment forward, I've brought what I learned with me and continue to refine and improve it. Over the last decade, I have helped hundreds of women accomplish their goals and dreams too, using this same method.

So, let's get this goal-setting party started!

Use the following steps to create your three goals for the next 90 days.

Step 1:

Revisit the dream life you manifested in Part I. Now, I want you to think about your current life. Envision that gap between where you are now and where you want to be. Now that you can see the gap, what are three things you can either add, change, remove, or make better **in the next 90 days** that will move the needle closer to that dream life?

For example, if you dream of being a millionaire and you currently have $100 in the bank account, you might write down "enroll in a wealth building course online", "cut out unnecessary expenses", or "start a side hustle to increase my income."

The key here is *not* to get overwhelmed by the end goal, but instead to focus on the next realistic step *for you* to achieve in 90 days.

Keep in mind that realistic means something different to all of us. Your next step will vary widely on your current state in life. Don't compare your journey or allow for those things to become excuses as to why you can't make progress. A next step is always available if we decide to take it.

What are three things you can realistically add, change, remove, or make better **in the next 90 days** that will move the needle closer to your dream life that you manifested in Part I?

1._____

_____

2._____

_____

3._____

_____

Step 2:

Turn each of those three things you just listed into a SMAART Goal.

What's a SMAART Goal?

I'm so glad you asked!

I don't do anything traditional, so I've taken the well-known SMART Goal outline and added a BEAM Life twist to it.

Here's what SMAART means:

Specific — Call out and name exactly what you want to do.

Measurable — How will you measure it?

Aligned — Is this desire in alignment with the dream life you manifested in Part I?

Achievable — Is this possible to achieve?

Results-oriented — What are the results that this will create in your life? This is the heart of the goal.

Time-based — By when will you achieve this goal? (I already gave you this one: 90 days!)

You see, before this step, you only had a wish, not a goal. A SMAART Goal gives us the ability to verify if what we say we want is clear and possible to attain. Think of it as a checks and balances system created to ensure your success.

Here's an example of how to build a SMAART Goal:

Example goal before SMAART criteria: *I want to be wealthier.*

The example above might be how your goals currently look. The problem is that this is too broad of a goal, and it could be achieved with a variety of different approaches or action steps. For example, in order to become wealthier, one could decide to add to their savings or investments, reduce spending, start a side hustle, etc. So, let's set into SMAART-ifying this goal.

1. Adding in Specific:

To improve this example, I would choose "increase my monthly income" to the goal as a way to become wealthier. I would also change the wording from "I want to be" to "I will become." This slight shift in language builds confidence as well as the way our brain approaches and responds to the goal.

Finally, It's also important to indicate how you plan to do the goal. For this example, I might add "by becoming a ride share driver on the weekends."

Up to this point, we've added our "Specific" criteria—but there's still more to do to create a true SMAART Goal.

> **Example after adding Specific:** *I will increase my net monthly income by becoming a ride share driver on the weekends.*

2. Adding in Measurable:

After adding the specific goal of increasing monthly income, you now have to determine how you will *measure* that. In the process of achieving any goal, knowing where you're currently at and how you will calculate change is important.

> **Example after adding Measurable:** *I will increase my net monthly income from $6,000 to $7,000 by becoming a ride share driver on the weekends. I will measure my progress by keeping track of my income and expenses on a spreadsheet.*

3. Adding in Aligned:

After knowing how you will measure your goal, ask yourself how *aligned* your new goal is to the dream life you manifested in Part I.

For example, at this point in the process, I would ask myself, "Does increasing my net monthly income from $6,000 to $7,000 get me closer to the dream life I desire and deserve?"

If the answer is "No," then I highly suggest starting the process over by building a new goal until you can answer the question with a *"Hell yes!"*

> **Example after adding Aligned:** Hell yes, *increasing my net monthly income from $6,000 to $7,000 by becoming a ride share driver on the weekends directly aligns with my dream life. I will measure my progress by keeping track of my income and expenses on a spreadsheet.*

4. Adding in Achievable:

Now that you are dialed in to the specifics and your alignment, we need to make sure you can *achieve* this in 90 days. Achieve can either mean:

Do I have the ability, tools, resources, time, etc. to achieve this goal in 90 days?

Or:

Is this goal not challenging enough, and can I do more in 90 days?

In this scenario, I reviewed my history, current opportunities, and how much ride share drivers can make, and I realized I was capable of achieving more. Turns out, I'm able to make closer to $8,000.

> **Example after adding Achievable:** Hell yes, *increasing my net monthly income from $6,000 to $8,000 by becoming a ride share driver on the weekends directly aligns with my dream life. I will measure my progress by keeping track of my income and expenses on a spreadsheet.*

5. Adding in Results-oriented:

This next part is my favorite. As I mentioned above, this is the heart of the goal-setting process. This is all about what achieving this goal will do for your life and how it will make you feel. It talks about what the *result* will be in your life. In other words, it's your *why*, and it will serve as a motivating reminder whenever you feel frustrated or get stopped by obstacles or self-doubt.

> **Example after adding Results-oriented:** Hell yes, *increasing my net monthly income from $6,000 to $8,000 by becoming a ride share driver on the weekends directly aligns*

with my dream life. I will measure my progress by keeping track of my income and expenses on a spreadsheet. Increasing my income is important to me, because I will be able to save for my child's fund and pay off all my debt. Being able to accomplish these things will bring me more joy and fulfillment.

6. Adding in Time-based:

The last part of building your goal is setting a deadline and making it all *time-based*. Without a deadline, you are left with an open-ended goal, which is one of the top reasons goals are not achieved. *In this journal, you will use 90 days from now as your deadline.*

> **Example after adding Time-based:** Hell yes, *in 90 days (insert date), increasing my net monthly income from $6,000 to $8,000 by becoming a ride share driver on the weekends directly aligns with my dream life. I will measure my progress by keeping track of my income and expenses on a spreadsheet. Increasing my income is important to me, because I will be able to save for my child's fund and pay off all my debt. Being able to accomplish these things will bring me more joy and fulfillment.*

For a more general template of this process, your goal should read something like this once you're done with the SMAART process:

Hell yes, in 90 days _____(insert date), I will _____ by doing _____. I will use _____ to track my progress. By accomplishing this goal, I will be able to do _____, and _____.

Now it's your turn! Using the steps and the example above, write down your three SMAART Goals for the next 90 days. Remember to use "I will" instead of "I want":

Goal 1:

_____

_____

_____

_____

Goal 2:

_____

_____

_____

_____

Goal 3:

_____

_____

_____

_____

Before moving on to the next step, read through each of your goals one more time. Are they specific, measurable, aligned, achievable, results-oriented, and time-based?

If you're unsure, connect with someone in the Facebook community group and ask for support and feedback.

Step 3:

Accountability is *everything*, so share your three SMAART Goals in the community Facebook group! There's power in saying and claiming what you want out loud and finding other women to join and support you.

PART III: STRATEGIZE

This part is about the dreaming meeting the doing. In other words, this will cover the *how* and *when* of your goals. Up until this point, you should've:

1. Manifested your dream life
2. Chosen three things to focus on over the next 90 days to bring you closer to your dream goals
3. Turned those three things into SMAART Goals

If you can successfully check off those items, then you're in the right place; if not, it's highly recommended you go back and follow the steps in order.

Next, we're going to do what I call BEAM Bricks.

I call them bricks because we are putting together the framework to build the literal foundation of your personal dream life. I don't know much about building a house, but I do know that you can't build anything without a foundation!

We will begin the process by mapping the three SMAART Goals you wrote down in Part II onto the next 90 days. Doing this will help you to organize and prioritize your actions so that you can accomplish your goals with confidence and ease!

Check out the graphic below which helps demonstrate how this will work:

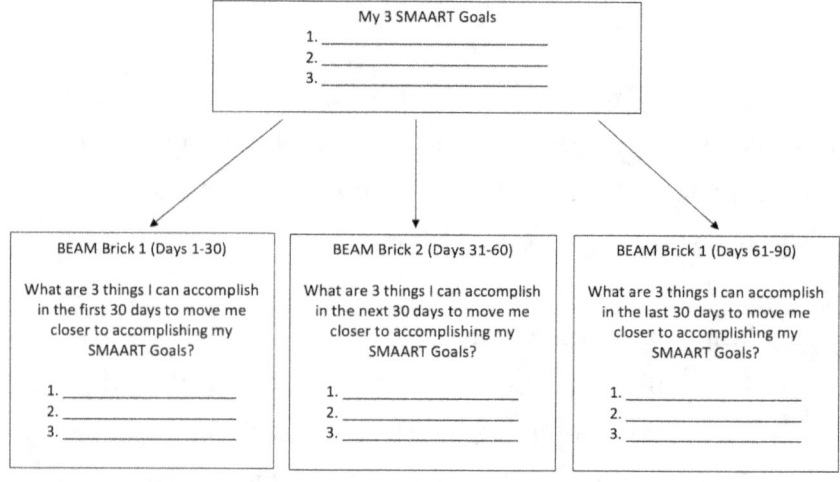

Don't try to fill in this graphic; it's just a representation of the flow of this process. Using the above, you can see in a visual way the growth you're about to experience over the next 90 days.

Once you have your own BEAM Bricks filled out, you're ready to move on to Part IV, where we will break each of these BEAM Bricks down even further.

PART IV: TAKE ACTION

The time has come where you get to press *go* and start creating your dream life. In the following pages, you will find daily journal prompts and an opportunity to break down each of the three **BEAM Bricks**.

The format and prompts for how you will do this is on the next page:

BRICK 1:

The dates for Brick 1 are _____ (today's date) _____ (30 days from today).

What are 3 things I can do in Brick 1 (Days 1-30) that will move me closer to my dream life?

_____

_____

_____

_____

_____

_____

_____

What tools, people, or resources do I need to make it happen?

_____

_____

_____

_____

_____

Who will I call if I get stuck or off-track?

_____

_____

_____

_____

What are some things that might get in my way?

_____

_____

_____

_____

_____

_____

_____

_____

How will I feel in 30 days after accomplishing these things?

_____

_____

_____

_____

_____

_____

_____

How will I celebrate taking action and making these changes?

_____

_____

_____

_____

_____

_____

_____

Though you'll only fill out each of the BEAM Bricks once, next you'll use journaling as a way to keep yourself account-able and on-track towards your goals. The template for these journal entries is simple, as you will see on the next page.

At the end of the 30 day process, if you've followed all the steps and kept yourself accountable, you will have accom-plished one part of your framework to one of your SMAART Goals! Once you've done that, do a quick reflection on the process of building your goals using the prompts at the end of each BEAM Brick.

Day 1

Today's Date:

Morning Reflections:

Today, I'm grateful for:

1._____

2._____

3._____

Today, I'm inviting _____ into my life.

Today I release control of:

_____

_____

_____

My main intention or focus for today is:

_____

_____

_____

Today is great, because:

_____

_____

Evening:

What's one thing I did today to make progress towards my goals?

_____

_____

_____

How did I get it right today?

_____

_____

_____

What do I release judgement on myself for?

_____

_____

_____

What made me BEAM today?

_____

_____

_____

End of day thoughts or highlights:

_____

_____

_____

_____

_____

Day 2

Today's Date:

Morning Reflections:

Today, I'm grateful for:

1._____

2._____

3._____

Today, I'm inviting _____ into my life.

Today I release control of:

_____

_____

_____

My main intention or focus for today is:

_____

_____

_____

Today is great, because:

_____

_____

Evening:

What's one thing I did today to make progress towards my goals?

_____

_____

_____

How did I get it right today?

_____

_____

_____

What do I release judgement on myself for?

_____

_____

_____

What made me BEAM today?

_____

_____

_____

End of day thoughts or highlights:

_____

_____

_____

_____

Day 3

Today's Date:

Morning Reflections:

Today, I'm grateful for:

1._____

2._____

3._____

Today, I'm inviting _____ into my life.

Today I release control of:

_____

_____

_____

My main intention or focus for today is:

_____

_____

_____

Today is great, because:

_____

_____

Evening:

What's one thing I did today to make progress towards my goals?

_____

_____

_____

How did I get it right today?

_____

_____

_____

What do I release judgement on myself for?

_____

_____

_____

What made me BEAM today?

_____

_____

_____

End of day thoughts or highlights:

_____

_____

_____

_____

_____

Day 4

Today's Date:

Morning Reflections:

Today, I'm grateful for:

1._____

2._____

3._____

Today, I'm inviting _____ into my life.

Today I release control of:

_____

_____

_____

My main intention or focus for today is:

_____

_____

_____

Today is great, because:

_____

_____

Evening:

What's one thing I did today to make progress towards my goals?

_____

_____

_____

How did I get it right today?

_____

_____

_____

What do I release judgement on myself for?

_____

_____

_____

What made me BEAM today?

_____

_____

_____

End of day thoughts or highlights:

_____

_____

_____

_____

_____

Day 5

Today's Date:

Morning Reflections:

Today, I'm grateful for:

1._____

2._____

3._____

Today, I'm inviting _____ into my life.

Today I release control of:

_____

_____

_____

My main intention or focus for today is:

_____

_____

_____

Today is great, because:

_____

_____

Evening:

What's one thing I did today to make progress towards my goals?

_____

_____

_____

How did I get it right today?

_____

_____

_____

What do I release judgement on myself for?

_____

_____

_____

What made me BEAM today?

_____

_____

_____

End of day thoughts or highlights:

_____

_____

_____

_____

_____

Day 6

Today's Date:

Morning Reflections:

Today, I'm grateful for:

1._____

2._____

3._____

Today, I'm inviting _____ into my life.

Today I release control of:

_____

_____

_____

My main intention or focus for today is:

_____

_____

_____

Today is great, because:

_____

_____

Evening:

What's one thing I did today to make progress towards my goals?

_____

_____

_____

How did I get it right today?

_____

_____

_____

What do I release judgement on myself for?

_____

_____

_____

What made me BEAM today?

_____

_____

_____

End of day thoughts or highlights:

_____

_____

_____

_____

Day 7

Today's Date:

Morning Reflections:

Today, I'm grateful for:

1._____

2._____

3._____

Today, I'm inviting _____ into my life.

Today I release control of:

_____

_____

_____

My main intention or focus for today is:

_____

_____

_____

Today is great, because:

_____

_____

Evening:

What's one thing I did today to make progress towards my goals?

_____

_____

_____

How did I get it right today?

_____

_____

_____

What do I release judgement on myself for?

_____

_____

_____

What made me BEAM today?

_____

_____

_____

End of day thoughts or highlights:

_____

_____

_____

_____

_____

Day 8

Today's Date:

Morning Reflections:

Today, I'm grateful for:

1._____

2._____

3._____

Today, I'm inviting _____ into my life.

Today I release control of:

_____

_____

_____

My main intention or focus for today is:

_____

_____

_____

Today is great, because:

_____

_____

Evening:

What's one thing I did today to make progress towards my goals?

_____

_____

_____

How did I get it right today?

_____

_____

_____

What do I release judgement on myself for?

_____

_____

_____

What made me BEAM today?

_____

_____

_____

End of day thoughts or highlights:

_____

_____

_____

_____

Day 9

Today's Date:

Morning Reflections:

Today, I'm grateful for:

1._____

2._____

3._____

Today, I'm inviting _____ into my life.

Today I release control of:

_____

_____

_____

My main intention or focus for today is:

_____

_____

_____

Today is great, because:

_____

_____

Evening:

What's one thing I did today to make progress towards my goals?

_____

_____

_____

How did I get it right today?

_____

_____

_____

What do I release judgement on myself for?

_____

_____

_____

What made me BEAM today?

_____

_____

_____

End of day thoughts or highlights:

_____

_____

_____

_____

_____

Day 10

Today's Date:

Morning Reflections:

Today, I'm grateful for:

1._____

2._____

3._____

Today, I'm inviting _____ into my life.

Today I release control of:

_____

_____

_____

My main intention or focus for today is:

_____

_____

_____

Today is great, because:

_____

_____

Evening:

What's one thing I did today to make progress towards my goals?

_____

_____

_____

How did I get it right today?

_____

_____

_____

What do I release judgement on myself for?

_____

_____

_____

What made me BEAM today?

_____

_____

_____

End of day thoughts or highlights:

_____

_____

_____

_____

Day 11

Today's Date:

Morning Reflections:

Today, I'm grateful for:

1._____

2._____

3._____

Today, I'm inviting _____ into my life.

Today I release control of:

_____

_____

_____

My main intention or focus for today is:

_____

_____

_____

Today is great, because:

_____

_____

Evening:

What's one thing I did today to make progress towards my goals?

_____

_____

_____

How did I get it right today?

_____

_____

_____

What do I release judgement on myself for?

_____

_____

_____

What made me BEAM today?

_____

_____

_____

End of day thoughts or highlights:

_____

_____

_____

_____

Day 12

Today's Date:

Morning Reflections:

Today, I'm grateful for:

1._____

2._____

3._____

Today, I'm inviting _____ into my life.

Today I release control of:

_____

_____

_____

My main intention or focus for today is:

_____

_____

_____

Today is great, because:

_____

_____

Evening:

What's one thing I did today to make progress towards my goals?

_____

_____

_____

How did I get it right today?

_____

_____

_____

What do I release judgement on myself for?

_____

_____

_____

What made me BEAM today?

_____

_____

_____

End of day thoughts or highlights:

_____

_____

_____

_____

_____

Day 13

Today's Date:

Morning Reflections:

Today, I'm grateful for:

1._____

2._____

3._____

Today, I'm inviting _____ into my life.

Today I release control of:

_____

_____

_____

My main intention or focus for today is:

_____

_____

_____

Today is great, because:

_____

_____

Evening:

What's one thing I did today to make progress towards my goals?

_____

_____

_____

How did I get it right today?

_____

_____

_____

What do I release judgement on myself for?

_____

_____

_____

What made me BEAM today?

_____

_____

_____

End of day thoughts or highlights:

_____

_____

_____

_____

Day 14

Today's Date:

Morning Reflections:

Today, I'm grateful for:

1._____

2._____

3._____

Today, I'm inviting _____ into my life.

Today I release control of:

_____

_____

_____

My main intention or focus for today is:

_____

_____

_____

Today is great, because:

_____

_____

Evening:

What's one thing I did today to make progress towards my goals?

_____

_____

_____

How did I get it right today?

_____

_____

_____

What do I release judgement on myself for?

_____

_____

_____

What made me BEAM today?

_____

_____

_____

End of day thoughts or highlights:

_____

_____

_____

_____

Day 15

Today's Date:

Morning Reflections:

Today, I'm grateful for:

1._____

2._____

3._____

Today, I'm inviting _____ into my life.

Today I release control of:

_____

_____

_____

My main intention or focus for today is:

_____

_____

_____

Today is great, because:

_____

_____

Evening:

What's one thing I did today to make progress towards my goals?

_____

_____

_____

How did I get it right today?

_____

_____

_____

What do I release judgement on myself for?

_____

_____

_____

What made me BEAM today?

_____

_____

_____

End of day thoughts or highlights:

_____

_____

_____

_____

Day 16

Today's Date:

Morning Reflections:

Today, I'm grateful for:

1._____

2._____

3._____

Today, I'm inviting _____ into my life.

Today I release control of:

_____

_____

_____

My main intention or focus for today is:

_____

_____

_____

Today is great, because:

_____

_____

Evening:

What's one thing I did today to make progress towards my goals?

_____

_____

_____

How did I get it right today?

_____

_____

_____

What do I release judgement on myself for?

_____

_____

_____

What made me BEAM today?

_____

_____

_____

End of day thoughts or highlights:

_____

_____

_____

_____

Day 17

Today's Date:

Morning Reflections:

Today, I'm grateful for:

1._____

2._____

3._____

Today, I'm inviting _____ into my life.

Today I release control of:

_____

_____

_____

My main intention or focus for today is:

_____

_____

_____

Today is great, because:

_____

_____

Evening:

What's one thing I did today to make progress towards my goals?

_____

_____

_____

How did I get it right today?

_____

_____

_____

What do I release judgement on myself for?

_____

_____

_____

What made me BEAM today?

_____

_____

_____

End of day thoughts or highlights:

_____

_____

_____

_____

Day 18

Today's Date:

Morning Reflections:

Today, I'm grateful for:

1._____

2._____

3._____

Today, I'm inviting _____ into my life.

Today I release control of:

_____

_____

_____

My main intention or focus for today is:

_____

_____

_____

Today is great, because:

_____

_____

Evening:

What's one thing I did today to make progress towards my goals?

_____

_____

_____

How did I get it right today?

_____

_____

_____

What do I release judgement on myself for?

_____

_____

_____

What made me BEAM today?

_____

_____

_____

End of day thoughts or highlights:

_____

_____

_____

_____

Day 19

Today's Date:

Morning Reflections:

Today, I'm grateful for:

1._____

2._____

3._____

Today, I'm inviting _____ into my life.

Today I release control of:

_____
_____
_____

My main intention or focus for today is:

_____
_____
_____

Today is great, because:

_____
_____

Evening:

What's one thing I did today to make progress towards my goals?

_____

_____

_____

How did I get it right today?

_____

_____

_____

What do I release judgement on myself for?

_____

_____

_____

What made me BEAM today?

_____

_____

_____

End of day thoughts or highlights:

_____

_____

_____

_____

Day 20

Today's Date:

Morning Reflections:

Today, I'm grateful for:

1._____

2._____

3._____

Today, I'm inviting _____ into my life.

Today I release control of:

_____

_____

_____

My main intention or focus for today is:

_____

_____

_____

Today is great, because:

_____

_____

Evening:

What's one thing I did today to make progress towards my goals?

_____

_____

_____

How did I get it right today?

_____

_____

_____

What do I release judgement on myself for?

_____

_____

_____

What made me BEAM today?

_____

_____

_____

End of day thoughts or highlights:

_____

_____

_____

_____

Day 21

Today's Date:

Morning Reflections:

Today, I'm grateful for:

1._____

2._____

3._____

Today, I'm inviting _____ into my life.

Today I release control of:

_____

_____

_____

My main intention or focus for today is:

_____

_____

_____

Today is great, because:

_____

_____

Evening:

What's one thing I did today to make progress towards my goals?

_____

_____

_____

How did I get it right today?

_____

_____

_____

What do I release judgement on myself for?

_____

_____

_____

What made me BEAM today?

_____

_____

_____

End of day thoughts or highlights:

_____

_____

_____

_____

Day 22

Today's Date:

Morning Reflections:

Today, I'm grateful for:

1._____

2._____

3._____

Today, I'm inviting _____ into my life.

Today I release control of:

_____

_____

_____

My main intention or focus for today is:

_____

_____

_____

Today is great, because:

_____

_____

Evening:

What's one thing I did today to make progress towards my goals?

_____

_____

_____

How did I get it right today?

_____

_____

_____

What do I release judgement on myself for?

_____

_____

_____

What made me BEAM today?

_____

_____

_____

End of day thoughts or highlights:

_____

_____

_____

_____

Day 23

Today's Date:

Morning Reflections:

Today, I'm grateful for:

1._____

2._____

3._____

Today, I'm inviting _____ into my life.

Today I release control of:

_____

_____

_____

My main intention or focus for today is:

_____

_____

_____

Today is great, because:

_____

_____

Evening:

What's one thing I did today to make progress towards my goals?

_____

_____

_____

How did I get it right today?

_____

_____

_____

What do I release judgement on myself for?

_____

_____

_____

What made me BEAM today?

_____

_____

_____

End of day thoughts or highlights:

_____

_____

_____

_____

Day 24

Today's Date:

Morning Reflections:

Today, I'm grateful for:

1._____

2._____

3._____

Today, I'm inviting _____ into my life.

Today I release control of:

_____

_____

_____

My main intention or focus for today is:

_____

_____

_____

Today is great, because:

_____

_____

Evening:

What's one thing I did today to make progress towards my goals?

_____

_____

_____

How did I get it right today?

_____

_____

_____

What do I release judgement on myself for?

_____

_____

_____

What made me BEAM today?

_____

_____

_____

End of day thoughts or highlights:

_____

_____

_____

_____

Day 25

Today's Date:

Morning Reflections:

Today, I'm grateful for:

1._____

2._____

3._____

Today, I'm inviting _____ into my life.

Today I release control of:

_____

_____

_____

My main intention or focus for today is:

_____

_____

_____

Today is great, because:

_____

_____

Evening:

What's one thing I did today to make progress towards my goals?

_____

_____

_____

How did I get it right today?

_____

_____

_____

What do I release judgement on myself for?

_____

_____

_____

What made me BEAM today?

_____

_____

_____

End of day thoughts or highlights:

_____

_____

_____

_____

Day 26

Today's Date:

Morning Reflections:

Today, I'm grateful for:

1._____

2._____

3._____

Today, I'm inviting _____ into my life.

Today I release control of:

_____

_____

_____

My main intention or focus for today is:

_____

_____

_____

Today is great, because:

_____

_____

Evening:

What's one thing I did today to make progress towards my goals?

_____

_____

_____

How did I get it right today?

_____

_____

_____

What do I release judgement on myself for?

_____

_____

_____

What made me BEAM today?

_____

_____

_____

End of day thoughts or highlights:

_____

_____

_____

_____

Day 27

Today's Date:

Morning Reflections:

Today, I'm grateful for:

1._____

2._____

3._____

Today, I'm inviting _____ into my life.

Today I release control of:

_____

_____

_____

My main intention or focus for today is:

_____

_____

_____

Today is great, because:

_____

_____

Evening:

What's one thing I did today to make progress towards my goals?

_____

_____

_____

How did I get it right today?

_____

_____

_____

What do I release judgement on myself for?

_____

_____

_____

What made me BEAM today?

_____

_____

_____

End of day thoughts or highlights:

_____

_____

_____

_____

Day 28

Today's Date:

Morning Reflections:

Today, I'm grateful for:

1._____

2._____

3._____

Today, I'm inviting _____ into my life.

Today I release control of:

_____

_____

_____

My main intention or focus for today is:

_____

_____

_____

Today is great, because:

_____

_____

Evening:

What's one thing I did today to make progress towards my goals?

_____

_____

_____

How did I get it right today?

_____

_____

_____

What do I release judgement on myself for?

_____

_____

_____

What made me BEAM today?

_____

_____

_____

End of day thoughts or highlights:

_____

_____

_____

_____

Day 29

Today's Date:

Morning Reflections:

Today, I'm grateful for:

1._____

2._____

3._____

Today, I'm inviting _____ into my life.

Today I release control of:

_____

_____

_____

My main intention or focus for today is:

_____

_____

_____

Today is great, because:

_____

_____

Evening:

What's one thing I did today to make progress towards my goals?

_____

_____

_____

How did I get it right today?

_____

_____

_____

What do I release judgement on myself for?

_____

_____

_____

What made me BEAM today?

_____

_____

_____

End of day thoughts or highlights:

_____

_____

_____

_____

Day 30

Today's Date:

Morning Reflections:

Today, I'm grateful for:

1._____

2._____

3._____

Today, I'm inviting _____ into my life.

Today I release control of:

_____

_____

_____

My main intention or focus for today is:

_____

_____

Today is great, because:

_____

_____

Evening:

What's one thing I did today to make progress towards my goals?

_____

_____

_____

How did I get it right today?

_____

_____

_____

What do I release judgement on myself for?

_____

_____

_____

What made me BEAM today?

_____

_____

_____

End of day thoughts or highlights:

_____

_____

_____

_____

BEAM BRICK 1 RECAP

What did I accomplish in the last 30 days?

_____
_____
_____
_____
_____
_____
_____

How does that make me feel?

_____
_____
_____
_____
_____
_____

What am I most proud of?

_____
_____
_____
_____

What will I do differently in BEAM Brick 2 (Days 31-60)?

_____

_____

_____

_____

_____

_____

Do I believe that what I want is possible? Why or why not?

_____

_____

_____

_____

_____

_____

And that's all there is to it! Next, repeat the same process for BEAM Bricks 2 and 3.

BRICK 2

The dates for Brick 2 are _____ (today's date) _____ (30 days from today).

What are 3 things I can do in Brick 2 (Days 31-60) that will move me closer to my dream life?

_____

_____

_____

_____

_____

_____

_____

What tools, people, or resources do I need to make it happen?

_____

_____

_____

_____

_____

Who will I call if I get stuck or off track?

_____

_____

_____

_____

What are some things that might get in my way?

_____
_____
_____
_____
_____
_____
_____

How will I feel in 30 days after accomplishing these things?

_____
_____
_____
_____
_____
_____
_____

How will I celebrate taking action and making these changes?

_____
_____
_____
_____
_____
_____
_____

Day 31

Today's Date:

Morning Reflections:

Today, I'm grateful for:

1._____

2._____

3._____

Today, I'm inviting _____ into my life.

Today I release control of:

_____

_____

_____

My main intention or focus for today is:

_____

_____

_____

Today is great, because:

_____

_____

Evening:

What's one thing I did today to make progress towards my goals?

_____

_____

_____

How did I get it right today?

_____

_____

_____

What do I release judgement on myself for?

_____

_____

_____

What made me BEAM today?

_____

_____

_____

End of day thoughts or highlights:

_____

_____

_____

_____

Day 32

Today's Date:

Morning Reflections:

Today, I'm grateful for:

1._____

2._____

3._____

Today, I'm inviting _____ into my life.

Today I release control of:

_____

_____

_____

My main intention or focus for today is:

_____

_____

_____

Today is great, because:

_____

_____

Evening:

What's one thing I did today to make progress towards my goals?

_____

_____

_____

How did I get it right today?

_____

_____

_____

What do I release judgement on myself for?

_____

_____

_____

What made me BEAM today?

_____

_____

_____

End of day thoughts or highlights:

_____

_____

_____

_____

Day 33

Today's Date:

Morning Reflections:

Today, I'm grateful for:

1._____

2._____

3._____

Today, I'm inviting _____ into my life.

Today I release control of:

_____

_____

_____

My main intention or focus for today is:

_____

_____

_____

Today is great, because:

_____

_____

Evening:

What's one thing I did today to make progress towards my goals?

_____

_____

_____

How did I get it right today?

_____

_____

_____

What do I release judgement on myself for?

_____

_____

_____

What made me BEAM today?

_____

_____

_____

End of day thoughts or highlights:

_____

_____

_____

_____

_____

Day 34

Today's Date:

Morning Reflections:

Today, I'm grateful for:

1._____

2._____

3._____

Today, I'm inviting _____ into my life.

Today I release control of:

_____

_____

_____

My main intention or focus for today is:

_____

_____

_____

Today is great, because:

_____

_____

Evening:

What's one thing I did today to make progress towards my goals?

_____

_____

_____

How did I get it right today?

_____

_____

_____

What do I release judgement on myself for?

_____

_____

_____

What made me BEAM today?

_____

_____

_____

End of day thoughts or highlights:

_____

_____

_____

_____

_____

Day 35

Today's Date:

Morning Reflections:

Today, I'm grateful for:

1._____

2._____

3._____

Today, I'm inviting _____ into my life.

Today I release control of:

_____
_____
_____

My main intention or focus for today is:

_____
_____
_____

Today is great, because:

_____
_____

Evening:

What's one thing I did today to make progress towards my goals?

_____

_____

_____

How did I get it right today?

_____

_____

_____

What do I release judgement on myself for?

_____

_____

_____

What made me BEAM today?

_____

_____

_____

End of day thoughts or highlights:

_____

_____

_____

_____

Day 36

Today's Date:

Morning Reflections:

Today, I'm grateful for:

1._____

2._____

3._____

Today, I'm inviting _____ into my life.

Today I release control of:

_____

_____

_____

My main intention or focus for today is:

_____

_____

_____

Today is great, because:

_____

_____

Evening:

What's one thing I did today to make progress towards my goals?

_____

_____

_____

How did I get it right today?

_____

_____

_____

What do I release judgement on myself for?

_____

_____

_____

What made me BEAM today?

_____

_____

_____

End of day thoughts or highlights:

_____

_____

_____

_____

Day 37

Today's Date:

Morning Reflections:

Today, I'm grateful for:

1._____

2._____

3._____

Today, I'm inviting _____ into my life.

Today I release control of:

_____

_____

_____

My main intention or focus for today is:

_____

_____

_____

Today is great, because:

_____

_____

Evening:

What's one thing I did today to make progress towards my goals?

_____

_____

_____

How did I get it right today?

_____

_____

_____

What do I release judgement on myself for?

_____

_____

_____

What made me BEAM today?

_____

_____

_____

End of day thoughts or highlights:

_____

_____

_____

_____

Day 38

Today's Date:

Morning Reflections:

Today, I'm grateful for:

1._____

2._____

3._____

Today, I'm inviting _____ into my life.

Today I release control of:

_____

_____

_____

My main intention or focus for today is:

_____

_____

_____

Today is great, because:

_____

_____

Evening:

What's one thing I did today to make progress towards my goals?

_____

_____

_____

How did I get it right today?

_____

_____

_____

What do I release judgement on myself for?

_____

_____

_____

What made me BEAM today?

_____

_____

_____

End of day thoughts or highlights:

_____

_____

_____

_____

Day 39

Today's Date:

Morning Reflections:

Today, I'm grateful for:

1._____

2._____

3._____

Today, I'm inviting _____ into my life.

Today I release control of:

_____

_____

_____

My main intention or focus for today is:

_____

_____

_____

Today is great, because:

_____

_____

Evening:

What's one thing I did today to make progress towards my goals?

_____

_____

_____

How did I get it right today?

_____

_____

_____

What do I release judgement on myself for?

_____

_____

_____

What made me BEAM today?

_____

_____

_____

End of day thoughts or highlights:

_____

_____

_____

_____

Day 40

Today's Date:

Morning Reflections:

Today, I'm grateful for:

1._____

2._____

3._____

Today, I'm inviting _____ into my life.

Today I release control of:

_____

_____

_____

My main intention or focus for today is:

_____

_____

_____

Today is great, because:

_____

_____

Evening:

What's one thing I did today to make progress towards my goals?

_____

_____

_____

How did I get it right today?

_____

_____

_____

What do I release judgement on myself for?

_____

_____

_____

What made me BEAM today?

_____

_____

_____

End of day thoughts or highlights:

_____

_____

_____

_____

Day 41

Today's Date:

Morning Reflections:

Today, I'm grateful for:

1._____

2._____

3._____

Today, I'm inviting _____ into my life.

Today I release control of:

_____

_____

_____

My main intention or focus for today is:

_____

_____

_____

Today is great, because:

_____

_____

Evening:

What's one thing I did today to make progress towards my goals?

_____

_____

_____

How did I get it right today?

_____

_____

_____

What do I release judgement on myself for?

_____

_____

_____

What made me BEAM today?

_____

_____

_____

End of day thoughts or highlights:

_____

_____

_____

_____

Day 42

Today's Date:

Morning Reflections:

Today, I'm grateful for:

1._____

2._____

3._____

Today, I'm inviting _____ into my life.

Today I release control of:

_____

_____

_____

My main intention or focus for today is:

_____

_____

_____

Today is great, because:

_____

_____

Evening:

What's one thing I did today to make progress towards my goals?

_____

_____

_____

How did I get it right today?

_____

_____

_____

What do I release judgement on myself for?

_____

_____

_____

What made me BEAM today?

_____

_____

_____

End of day thoughts or highlights:

_____

_____

_____

_____

Day 43

Today's Date:

Morning Reflections:

Today, I'm grateful for:

1._____

2._____

3._____

Today, I'm inviting _____ into my life.

Today I release control of:

_____

_____

_____

My main intention or focus for today is:

_____

_____

_____

Today is great, because:

_____

_____

Evening:

What's one thing I did today to make progress towards my goals?

_____

_____

_____

How did I get it right today?

_____

_____

_____

What do I release judgement on myself for?

_____

_____

_____

What made me BEAM today?

_____

_____

_____

End of day thoughts or highlights:

_____

_____

_____

_____

Day 44

Today's Date:

Morning Reflections:

Today, I'm grateful for:

1._____

2._____

3._____

Today, I'm inviting _____ into my life.

Today I release control of:

_____

_____

_____

My main intention or focus for today is:

_____

_____

_____

Today is great, because:

_____

_____

Evening:

What's one thing I did today to make progress towards my goals?

_____

_____

_____

How did I get it right today?

_____

_____

_____

What do I release judgement on myself for?

_____

_____

_____

What made me BEAM today?

_____

_____

_____

End of day thoughts or highlights:

_____

_____

_____

_____

Day 45

Today's Date:

Morning Reflections:

Today, I'm grateful for:

1._____

2._____

3._____

Today, I'm inviting _____ into my life.

Today I release control of:

_____

_____

_____

My main intention or focus for today is:

_____

_____

_____

Today is great, because:

_____

_____

Evening:

What's one thing I did today to make progress towards my goals?

_____

_____

_____

How did I get it right today?

_____

_____

_____

What do I release judgement on myself for?

_____

_____

_____

What made me BEAM today?

_____

_____

_____

End of day thoughts or highlights:

_____

_____

_____

_____

Day 46

Today's Date:

Morning Reflections:

Today, I'm grateful for:

1._____

2._____

3._____

Today, I'm inviting _____ into my life.

Today I release control of:

_____

_____

_____

My main intention or focus for today is:

_____

_____

_____

Today is great, because:

_____

_____

Evening:

What's one thing I did today to make progress towards my goals?

_____

_____

_____

How did I get it right today?

_____

_____

_____

What do I release judgement on myself for?

_____

_____

_____

What made me BEAM today?

_____

_____

_____

End of day thoughts or highlights:

_____

_____

_____

_____

_____

Day 47

Today's Date:

Morning Reflections:

Today, I'm grateful for:

1._____

2._____

3._____

Today, I'm inviting _____ into my life.

Today I release control of:

_____

_____

_____

My main intention or focus for today is:

_____

_____

_____

Today is great, because:

_____

_____

Evening:

What's one thing I did today to make progress towards my goals?

_____

_____

_____

How did I get it right today?

_____

_____

_____

What do I release judgement on myself for?

_____

_____

_____

What made me BEAM today?

_____

_____

_____

End of day thoughts or highlights:

_____

_____

_____

_____

Day 48

Today's Date:

Morning Reflections:

Today, I'm grateful for:

1._____

2._____

3._____

Today, I'm inviting _____ into my life.

Today I release control of:

_____

_____

_____

My main intention or focus for today is:

_____

_____

_____

Today is great, because:

_____

_____

Evening:

What's one thing I did today to make progress towards my goals?

_____

_____

_____

How did I get it right today?

_____

_____

_____

What do I release judgement on myself for?

_____

_____

_____

What made me BEAM today?

_____

_____

_____

End of day thoughts or highlights:

_____

_____

_____

_____

Day 49

Today's Date:

Morning Reflections:

Today, I'm grateful for:

1._____

2._____

3._____

Today, I'm inviting _____ into my life.

Today I release control of:

_____

_____

_____

My main intention or focus for today is:

_____

_____

_____

Today is great, because:

_____

_____

Evening:

What's one thing I did today to make progress towards my goals?

_____

_____

_____

How did I get it right today?

_____

_____

_____

What do I release judgement on myself for?

_____

_____

_____

What made me BEAM today?

_____

_____

_____

End of day thoughts or highlights:

_____

_____

_____

_____

Day 50

Today's Date:

Morning Reflections:

Today, I'm grateful for:

1._____

2._____

3._____

Today, I'm inviting _____ into my life.

Today I release control of:

_____

_____

_____

My main intention or focus for today is:

_____

_____

_____

Today is great, because:

_____

_____

Evening:

What's one thing I did today to make progress towards my goals?

_____

_____

_____

How did I get it right today?

_____

_____

_____

What do I release judgement on myself for?

_____

_____

_____

What made me BEAM today?

_____

_____

_____

End of day thoughts or highlights:

_____

_____

_____

_____

Day 51

Today's Date:

Morning Reflections:

Today, I'm grateful for:

1._____

2._____

3._____

Today, I'm inviting _____ into my life.

Today I release control of:

_____

_____

_____

My main intention or focus for today is:

_____

_____

_____

Today is great, because:

_____

_____

Evening:

What's one thing I did today to make progress towards my goals?

_____

_____

_____

How did I get it right today?

_____

_____

_____

What do I release judgement on myself for?

_____

_____

_____

What made me BEAM today?

_____

_____

_____

End of day thoughts or highlights:

_____

_____

_____

_____

Day 52

Today's Date:

Morning Reflections:

Today, I'm grateful for:

1._____

2._____

3._____

Today, I'm inviting _____ into my life.

Today I release control of:

_____

_____

_____

My main intention or focus for today is:

_____

_____

_____

Today is great, because:

_____

_____

Evening:

What's one thing I did today to make progress towards my goals?

_____

_____

_____

How did I get it right today?

_____

_____

_____

What do I release judgement on myself for?

_____

_____

_____

What made me BEAM today?

_____

_____

_____

End of day thoughts or highlights:

_____

_____

_____

_____

_____

Day 53

Today's Date:

Morning Reflections:

Today, I'm grateful for:

1._____

2._____

3._____

Today, I'm inviting _____ into my life.

Today I release control of:

_____

_____

_____

My main intention or focus for today is:

_____

_____

_____

Today is great, because:

_____

_____

Evening:

What's one thing I did today to make progress towards my goals?

_____

_____

_____

How did I get it right today?

_____

_____

_____

What do I release judgement on myself for?

_____

_____

_____

What made me BEAM today?

_____

_____

_____

End of day thoughts or highlights:

_____

_____

_____

_____

Day 54

Today's Date:

Morning Reflections:

Today, I'm grateful for:

1._____

2._____

3._____

Today, I'm inviting _____ into my life.

Today I release control of:

_____

_____

_____

My main intention or focus for today is:

_____

_____

_____

Today is great, because:

_____

_____

Evening:

What's one thing I did today to make progress towards my goals?

_____

_____

_____

How did I get it right today?

_____

_____

_____

What do I release judgement on myself for?

_____

_____

_____

What made me BEAM today?

_____

_____

_____

End of day thoughts or highlights:

_____

_____

_____

_____

Day 55

Today's Date:

Morning Reflections:

Today, I'm grateful for:

1._____

2._____

3._____

Today, I'm inviting _____ into my life.

Today I release control of:

_____

_____

_____

My main intention or focus for today is:

_____

_____

_____

Today is great, because:

_____

_____

Evening:

What's one thing I did today to make progress towards my goals?

_____

_____

_____

How did I get it right today?

_____

_____

_____

What do I release judgement on myself for?

_____

_____

_____

What made me BEAM today?

_____

_____

_____

End of day thoughts or highlights:

_____

_____

_____

_____

Day 56

Today's Date:

Morning Reflections:

Today, I'm grateful for:

1._____

2._____

3._____

Today, I'm inviting _____ into my life.

Today I release control of:

_____

_____

_____

My main intention or focus for today is:

_____

_____

_____

Today is great, because:

_____

_____

Evening:

What's one thing I did today to make progress towards my goals?

_____

_____

_____

How did I get it right today?

_____

_____

_____

What do I release judgement on myself for?

_____

_____

_____

What made me BEAM today?

_____

_____

_____

End of day thoughts or highlights:

_____

_____

_____

_____

Day 57

Today's Date:

Morning Reflections:

Today, I'm grateful for:

1._____

2._____

3._____

Today, I'm inviting _____ into my life.

Today I release control of:

_____

_____

_____

My main intention or focus for today is:

_____

_____

_____

Today is great, because:

_____

_____

Evening:

What's one thing I did today to make progress towards my goals?

_____

_____

_____

How did I get it right today?

_____

_____

_____

What do I release judgement on myself for?

_____

_____

_____

What made me BEAM today?

_____

_____

_____

End of day thoughts or highlights:

_____

_____

_____

_____

_____

Day 58

Today's Date:

Morning Reflections:

Today, I'm grateful for:

1._____

2._____

3._____

Today, I'm inviting _____ into my life.

Today I release control of:

_____

_____

_____

My main intention or focus for today is:

_____

_____

_____

Today is great, because:

_____

_____

Evening:

What's one thing I did today to make progress towards my goals?

_____

_____

_____

How did I get it right today?

_____

_____

_____

What do I release judgement on myself for?

_____

_____

_____

What made me BEAM today?

_____

_____

_____

End of day thoughts or highlights:

_____

_____

_____

_____

Day 59

Today's Date:

Morning Reflections:

Today, I'm grateful for:

1._____

2._____

3._____

Today, I'm inviting _____ into my life.

Today I release control of:

_____

_____

_____

My main intention or focus for today is:

_____

_____

_____

Today is great, because:

_____

_____

Evening:

What's one thing I did today to make progress towards my goals?

_____

_____

_____

How did I get it right today?

_____

_____

_____

What do I release judgement on myself for?

_____

_____

_____

What made me BEAM today?

_____

_____

_____

End of day thoughts or highlights:

_____

_____

_____

_____

Day 60

Today's Date:

Morning Reflections:

Today, I'm grateful for:

1._____

2._____

3._____

Today, I'm inviting _____ into my life.

Today I release control of:

_____
_____
_____

My main intention or focus for today is:

_____
_____
_____

Today is great, because:

_____
_____

Evening:

What's one thing I did today to make progress towards my goals?

_____

_____

_____

How did I get it right today?

_____

_____

_____

What do I release judgement on myself for?

_____

_____

_____

What made me BEAM today?

_____

_____

_____

End of day thoughts or highlights:

_____

_____

_____

_____

_____

BEAM BRICK 2 RECAP

What did I accomplish in the last 60 days?

_____

_____

_____

_____

_____

_____

_____

How does that make me feel?

_____

_____

_____

_____

_____

_____

What am I most proud of?

_____

_____

_____

_____

What will I do differently in BEAM Brick 3 (Days 61-90)?

_____

_____

_____

_____

_____

_____

Do I believe that what I want is possible? Why or why not?

_____

_____

_____

_____

_____

_____

BRICK 3

The dates for Brick 3 are _____ (today's date) _____ (30 days from today).

What are 3 things I can do in Brick 3 (Days 61-90) that will move me closer to my dream life?

_____

_____

_____

_____

_____

_____

_____

What tools, people, or resources do I need to make it happen?

_____

_____

_____

_____

_____

_____

Who will I call if I get stuck or off-track?

_____

_____

_____

_____

_____

What are some things that might get in my way?

_____

_____

_____

_____

_____

_____

_____

How will I feel in 30 days after accomplishing these things?

_____

_____

_____

_____

_____

_____

_____

How will I celebrate taking action and making these changes?

_____

_____

_____

_____

_____

_____

_____

Day 61

Today's Date:

Morning Reflections:

Today, I'm grateful for:

1._____

2._____

3._____

Today, I'm inviting _____ into my life.

Today I release control of:

_____

_____

_____

My main intention or focus for today is:

_____

_____

_____

Today is great, because:

_____

_____

Evening:

What's one thing I did today to make progress towards my goals?

_____

_____

_____

How did I get it right today?

_____

_____

_____

What do I release judgement on myself for?

_____

_____

_____

What made me BEAM today?

_____

_____

_____

End of day thoughts or highlights:

_____

_____

_____

_____

_____

Day 62

Today's Date:

Morning Reflections:

Today, I'm grateful for:

1._____

2._____

3._____

Today, I'm inviting _____ into my life.

Today I release control of:

_____

_____

_____

My main intention or focus for today is:

_____

_____

_____

Today is great, because:

_____

_____

Evening:

What's one thing I did today to make progress towards my goals?

_____

_____

_____

How did I get it right today?

_____

_____

_____

What do I release judgement on myself for?

_____

_____

_____

What made me BEAM today?

_____

_____

_____

End of day thoughts or highlights:

_____

_____

_____

_____

Day 63

Today's Date:

Morning Reflections:

Today, I'm grateful for:

1._____

2._____

3._____

Today, I'm inviting _____ into my life.

Today I release control of:

_____

_____

_____

My main intention or focus for today is:

_____

_____

_____

Today is great, because:

_____

_____

Evening:

What's one thing I did today to make progress towards my goals?

_____

_____

_____

How did I get it right today?

_____

_____

_____

What do I release judgement on myself for?

_____

_____

_____

What made me BEAM today?

_____

_____

_____

End of day thoughts or highlights:

_____

_____

_____

_____

Day 64

Today's Date:

Morning Reflections:

Today, I'm grateful for:

1._____

2._____

3._____

Today, I'm inviting _____ into my life.

Today I release control of:

_____

_____

_____

My main intention or focus for today is:

_____

_____

_____

Today is great, because:

_____

_____

Evening:

What's one thing I did today to make progress towards my goals?

_____

_____

_____

How did I get it right today?

_____

_____

_____

What do I release judgement on myself for?

_____

_____

_____

What made me BEAM today?

_____

_____

_____

End of day thoughts or highlights:

_____

_____

_____

_____

Day 65

Today's Date:

Morning Reflections:

Today, I'm grateful for:

1._____

2._____

3._____

Today, I'm inviting _____ into my life.

Today I release control of:

_____

_____

_____

My main intention or focus for today is:

_____

_____

_____

Today is great, because:

_____

_____

Evening:

What's one thing I did today to make progress towards my goals?

_____

_____

_____

How did I get it right today?

_____

_____

_____

What do I release judgement on myself for?

_____

_____

_____

What made me BEAM today?

_____

_____

_____

End of day thoughts or highlights:

_____

_____

_____

_____

_____

Day 66

Today's Date:

Morning Reflections:

Today, I'm grateful for:

1._____

2._____

3._____

Today, I'm inviting _____ into my life.

Today I release control of:

_____

_____

_____

My main intention or focus for today is:

_____

_____

_____

Today is great, because:

_____

_____

Evening:

What's one thing I did today to make progress towards my goals?

_____

_____

_____

How did I get it right today?

_____

_____

_____

What do I release judgement on myself for?

_____

_____

_____

What made me BEAM today?

_____

_____

_____

End of day thoughts or highlights:

_____

_____

_____

_____

Day 67

Today's Date:

Morning Reflections:

Today, I'm grateful for:

1._____

2._____

3._____

Today, I'm inviting _____ into my life.

Today I release control of:

_____

_____

_____

My main intention or focus for today is:

_____

_____

_____

Today is great, because:

_____

_____

Evening:

What's one thing I did today to make progress towards my goals?

_____

_____

_____

How did I get it right today?

_____

_____

_____

What do I release judgement on myself for?

_____

_____

_____

What made me BEAM today?

_____

_____

_____

End of day thoughts or highlights:

_____

_____

_____

_____

Day 68

Today's Date:

Morning Reflections:

Today, I'm grateful for:

1._____

2._____

3._____

Today, I'm inviting _____ into my life.

Today I release control of:

_____

_____

_____

My main intention or focus for today is:

_____

_____

_____

Today is great, because:

_____

_____

Evening:

What's one thing I did today to make progress towards my goals?

_____

_____

_____

How did I get it right today?

_____

_____

_____

What do I release judgement on myself for?

_____

_____

_____

What made me BEAM today?

_____

_____

_____

End of day thoughts or highlights:

_____

_____

_____

_____

Day 69

Today's Date:

Morning Reflections:

Today, I'm grateful for:

1._____

2._____

3._____

Today, I'm inviting _____ into my life.

Today I release control of:

_____

_____

_____

My main intention or focus for today is:

_____

_____

_____

Today is great, because:

_____

_____

Evening:

What's one thing I did today to make progress towards my goals?

_____

_____

_____

How did I get it right today?

_____

_____

_____

What do I release judgement on myself for?

_____

_____

_____

What made me BEAM today?

_____

_____

_____

End of day thoughts or highlights:

_____

_____

_____

_____

Day 70

Today's Date:

Morning Reflections:

Today, I'm grateful for:

1._____

2._____

3._____

Today, I'm inviting _____ into my life.

Today I release control of:

_____

_____

_____

My main intention or focus for today is:

_____

_____

_____

Today is great, because:

_____

_____

Evening:

What's one thing I did today to make progress towards my goals?

_____

_____

_____

How did I get it right today?

_____

_____

_____

What do I release judgement on myself for?

_____

_____

_____

What made me BEAM today?

_____

_____

_____

End of day thoughts or highlights:

_____

_____

_____

_____

_____

Day 71

Today's Date:

Morning Reflections:

Today, I'm grateful for:

1._____

2._____

3._____

Today, I'm inviting _____ into my life.

Today I release control of:

_____

_____

_____

My main intention or focus for today is:

_____

_____

_____

Today is great, because:

_____

_____

Evening:

What's one thing I did today to make progress towards my goals?

_____

_____

_____

How did I get it right today?

_____

_____

_____

What do I release judgement on myself for?

_____

_____

_____

What made me BEAM today?

_____

_____

_____

End of day thoughts or highlights:

_____

_____

_____

_____

_____

Day 72

Today's Date:

Morning Reflections:

Today, I'm grateful for:

1._____

2._____

3._____

Today, I'm inviting _____ into my life.

Today I release control of:

_____

_____

_____

My main intention or focus for today is:

_____

_____

_____

Today is great, because:

_____

_____

Evening:

What's one thing I did today to make progress towards my goals?

_____

_____

_____

How did I get it right today?

_____

_____

_____

What do I release judgement on myself for?

_____

_____

_____

What made me BEAM today?

_____

_____

_____

End of day thoughts or highlights:

_____

_____

_____

_____

Day 73

Today's Date:

Morning Reflections:

Today, I'm grateful for:

1._____

2._____

3._____

Today, I'm inviting _____ into my life.

Today I release control of:

_____

_____

_____

My main intention or focus for today is:

_____

_____

_____

Today is great, because:

_____

_____

Evening:

What's one thing I did today to make progress towards my goals?

_____

_____

_____

How did I get it right today?

_____

_____

_____

What do I release judgement on myself for?

_____

_____

_____

What made me BEAM today?

_____

_____

_____

End of day thoughts or highlights:

_____

_____

_____

_____

Day 74

Today's Date:

Morning Reflections:

Today, I'm grateful for:

1._____

2._____

3._____

Today, I'm inviting _____ into my life.

Today I release control of:

_____

_____

_____

My main intention or focus for today is:

_____

_____

_____

Today is great, because:

_____

_____

Evening:

What's one thing I did today to make progress towards my goals?

_____

_____

_____

How did I get it right today?

_____

_____

_____

What do I release judgement on myself for?

_____

_____

_____

What made me BEAM today?

_____

_____

_____

End of day thoughts or highlights:

_____

_____

_____

_____

Day 75

Today's Date:

Morning Reflections:

Today, I'm grateful for:

1._____

2._____

3._____

Today, I'm inviting _____ into my life.

Today I release control of:

_____

_____

_____

My main intention or focus for today is:

_____

_____

_____

Today is great, because:

_____

_____

Evening:

What's one thing I did today to make progress towards my goals?

_____

_____

_____

How did I get it right today?

_____

_____

_____

What do I release judgement on myself for?

_____

_____

_____

What made me BEAM today?

_____

_____

_____

End of day thoughts or highlights:

_____

_____

_____

_____

Day 76

Today's Date:

Morning Reflections:

Today, I'm grateful for:

1._____

2._____

3._____

Today, I'm inviting _____ into my life.

Today I release control of:

_____

_____

_____

My main intention or focus for today is:

_____

_____

_____

Today is great, because:

_____

_____

Evening:

What's one thing I did today to make progress towards my goals?

_____

_____

_____

How did I get it right today?

_____

_____

_____

What do I release judgement on myself for?

_____

_____

_____

What made me BEAM today?

_____

_____

_____

End of day thoughts or highlights:

_____

_____

_____

_____

Day 77

Today's Date:

Morning Reflections:

Today, I'm grateful for:

1._____

2._____

3._____

Today, I'm inviting _____ into my life.

Today I release control of:

_____

_____

_____

My main intention or focus for today is:

_____

_____

_____

Today is great, because:

_____

_____

Evening:

What's one thing I did today to make progress towards my goals?

_____

_____

_____

How did I get it right today?

_____

_____

_____

What do I release judgement on myself for?

_____

_____

_____

What made me BEAM today?

_____

_____

_____

End of day thoughts or highlights:

_____

_____

_____

_____

_____

Day 78

Today's Date:

Morning Reflections:

Today, I'm grateful for:

1._____

2._____

3._____

Today, I'm inviting _____ into my life.

Today I release control of:

_____

_____

_____

My main intention or focus for today is:

_____

_____

_____

Today is great, because:

_____

_____

Evening:

What's one thing I did today to make progress towards my goals?

_____

_____

_____

How did I get it right today?

_____

_____

_____

What do I release judgement on myself for?

_____

_____

_____

What made me BEAM today?

_____

_____

_____

End of day thoughts or highlights:

_____

_____

_____

_____

_____

Day 79

Today's Date:

Morning Reflections:

Today, I'm grateful for:

1._____

2._____

3._____

Today, I'm inviting _____ into my life.

Today I release control of:

_____

_____

_____

My main intention or focus for today is:

_____

_____

_____

Today is great, because:

_____

_____

Evening:

What's one thing I did today to make progress towards my goals?

_____

_____

_____

How did I get it right today?

_____

_____

_____

What do I release judgement on myself for?

_____

_____

_____

What made me BEAM today?

_____

_____

_____

End of day thoughts or highlights:

_____

_____

_____

_____

Day 80

Today's Date:

Morning Reflections:

Today, I'm grateful for:

1._____

2._____

3._____

Today, I'm inviting _____ into my life.

Today I release control of:

_____

_____

_____

My main intention or focus for today is:

_____

_____

_____

Today is great, because:

_____

_____

Evening:

What's one thing I did today to make progress towards my goals?

_____

_____

_____

How did I get it right today?

_____

_____

_____

What do I release judgement on myself for?

_____

_____

_____

What made me BEAM today?

_____

_____

_____

End of day thoughts or highlights:

_____

_____

_____

_____

_____

Day 81

Today's Date:

Morning Reflections:

Today, I'm grateful for:

1._____

2._____

3._____

Today, I'm inviting _____ into my life.

Today I release control of:

_____

_____

_____

My main intention or focus for today is:

_____

_____

_____

Today is great, because:

_____

_____

Evening:

What's one thing I did today to make progress towards my goals?

_____

_____

_____

How did I get it right today?

_____

_____

_____

What do I release judgement on myself for?

_____

_____

_____

What made me BEAM today?

_____

_____

_____

End of day thoughts or highlights:

_____

_____

_____

_____

Day 82

Today's Date:

Morning Reflections:

Today, I'm grateful for:

1._____

2._____

3._____

Today, I'm inviting _____ into my life.

Today I release control of:

_____

_____

_____

My main intention or focus for today is:

_____

_____

_____

Today is great, because:

_____

_____

Evening:

What's one thing I did today to make progress towards my goals?

_____

_____

_____

How did I get it right today?

_____

_____

_____

What do I release judgement on myself for?

_____

_____

_____

What made me BEAM today?

_____

_____

_____

End of day thoughts or highlights:

_____

_____

_____

_____

Day 83

Today's Date:

Morning Reflections:

Today, I'm grateful for:

1._____

2._____

3._____

Today, I'm inviting _____ into my life.

Today I release control of:

_____

_____

_____

My main intention or focus for today is:

_____

_____

_____

Today is great, because:

_____

_____

Evening:

What's one thing I did today to make progress towards my goals?

_____

_____

_____

How did I get it right today?

_____

_____

_____

What do I release judgement on myself for?

_____

_____

_____

What made me BEAM today?

_____

_____

_____

End of day thoughts or highlights:

_____

_____

_____

_____

Day 84

Today's Date:

Morning Reflections:

Today, I'm grateful for:

1._____

2._____

3._____

Today, I'm inviting _____ into my life.

Today I release control of:

_____

_____

_____

My main intention or focus for today is:

_____

_____

_____

Today is great, because:

_____

_____

Evening:

What's one thing I did today to make progress towards my goals?

_____

_____

_____

How did I get it right today?

_____

_____

_____

What do I release judgement on myself for?

_____

_____

_____

What made me BEAM today?

_____

_____

_____

End of day thoughts or highlights:

_____

_____

_____

_____

Day 85

Today's Date:

Morning Reflections:

Today, I'm grateful for:

1._____

2._____

3._____

Today, I'm inviting _____ into my life.

Today I release control of:

_____

_____

_____

My main intention or focus for today is:

_____

_____

_____

Today is great, because:

_____

_____

Evening:

What's one thing I did today to make progress towards my goals?

_____

_____

_____

How did I get it right today?

_____

_____

_____

What do I release judgement on myself for?

_____

_____

_____

What made me BEAM today?

_____

_____

_____

End of day thoughts or highlights:

_____

_____

_____

_____

Day 86

Today's Date:

Morning Reflections:

Today, I'm grateful for:

1._____

2._____

3._____

Today, I'm inviting _____ into my life.

Today I release control of:

_____

_____

_____

My main intention or focus for today is:

_____

_____

_____

Today is great, because:

_____

_____

Evening:

What's one thing I did today to make progress towards my goals?

_____

_____

_____

How did I get it right today?

_____

_____

_____

What do I release judgement on myself for?

_____

_____

_____

What made me BEAM today?

_____

_____

_____

End of day thoughts or highlights:

_____

_____

_____

_____

Day 87

Today's Date:

Morning Reflections:

Today, I'm grateful for:

1._____

2._____

3._____

Today, I'm inviting _____ into my life.

Today I release control of:

_____

_____

_____

My main intention or focus for today is:

_____

_____

_____

Today is great, because:

_____

_____

Evening:

What's one thing I did today to make progress towards my goals?

_____

_____

_____

How did I get it right today?

_____

_____

_____

What do I release judgement on myself for?

_____

_____

_____

What made me BEAM today?

_____

_____

_____

End of day thoughts or highlights:

_____

_____

_____

_____

Day 88

Today's Date:

Morning Reflections:

Today, I'm grateful for:

1._____

2._____

3._____

Today, I'm inviting _____ into my life.

Today I release control of:

_____

_____

_____

My main intention or focus for today is:

_____

_____

_____

Today is great, because:

_____

_____

Evening:

What's one thing I did today to make progress towards my goals?

_____

_____

_____

How did I get it right today?

_____

_____

_____

What do I release judgement on myself for?

_____

_____

_____

What made me BEAM today?

_____

_____

_____

End of day thoughts or highlights:

_____

_____

_____

_____

Day 89

Today's Date:

Morning Reflections:

Today, I'm grateful for:

1._____

2._____

3._____

Today, I'm inviting _____ into my life.

Today I release control of:

_____

_____

_____

My main intention or focus for today is:

_____

_____

_____

Today is great, because:

_____

_____

Evening:

What's one thing I did today to make progress towards my goals?

_____

_____

_____

How did I get it right today?

_____

_____

_____

What do I release judgement on myself for?

_____

_____

_____

What made me BEAM today?

_____

_____

_____

End of day thoughts or highlights:

_____

_____

_____

_____

Day 90

Today's Date:

Morning Reflections:

Today, I'm grateful for:

1._____

2._____

3._____

Today, I'm inviting _____ into my life.

Today I release control of:

_____
_____
_____

My main intention or focus for today is:

_____
_____
_____

Today is great, because:

_____
_____

Evening:

What's one thing I did today to make progress towards my goals?

_____

_____

_____

How did I get it right today?

_____

_____

_____

What do I release judgement on myself for?

_____

_____

_____

What made me BEAM today?

_____

_____

_____

End of day thoughts or highlights:

_____

_____

_____

_____

BEAM BRICK 3 RECAP

What did I accomplish in the last 90 days?

_____

_____

_____

_____

_____

_____

How does that make me feel?

_____

_____

_____

_____

_____

_____

What am I most proud of?

_____

_____

_____

_____

_____

Do I believe that what I want is possible? Why or why not?

_____

_____

_____

_____

_____

_____

_____

Thoughts and reflections after 90 days of living with intention:

_____

_____

_____

_____

_____

_____

_____

_____

_____

_____

_____

_____

_____

_____

PART V: CELEBRATE

Congrats, babe!

You've made it to the end of your 90-day commitments, and it's time to celebrate. Acknowledging yourself for what you've accomplished is a crucial part of your future success. It's easy to keep your head down and look for the next goal, but I beg you, don't let this moment pass you by unnoticed.

I want to make sure to point out that it's not about whether or not you completed the goal perfectly, but more about whether you showed up for yourself and took action towards a life that has been waiting for you. That perfectionist bullshit is who you *were*—it is so 90 days ago!

When I say the word "celebrate," it may bring up a few expectations, since we've been conditioned as a society that it means spend money. I want to reassure you that you can acknowledge you badass self without spending a dime.

Here are some of my clients' favorite ways to celebrate that don't cost much:

- Call or meet up with a friend
- Get cozy and read a book
- Declutter
- Make someone smile or lend them a hand
- Listen to a podcast (I hear The BEAM Life is a great one!)
- Connect with your partner or significant other
- Cook your favorite meal
- Take a nap
- Build a playlist
- Soak your feet in warm water
- Light incense or candles
- Do something creative like paint, draw, knit, make music, etc.
- Cuddle with your pets
- Mindfully take a bubble bath
- Give yourself or ask for a massage
- Take a free online workout yoga or meditation class
- Call or connect with a family member
- Take a walk and be aware of your surroundings
- Turn your phone off
- Go through old photo albums
- Put on your favorite tunes and dance
- Watch your favorite movie or show
- Get playful and go to a park
- Write a letter to your future self
- Make a vision board

These are all just ideas, and of course if you want to celebrate by taking a first class trip around the world, don't let me stop you! Share in the group how you decided to celebrate, because we want to celebrate you too!

I used the exact strategy that I just taught you to get on my feet after going through a rough divorce in September 2019. I made the decision to not only separate from my then-husband, but also our successful family fitness business. This was, as we all know, followed by a global pandemic five months later.

Starting over at the age of 33 as a single mother was over-whelming to say the least. However, I knew that I had a tried-and-true process I could rely on to get me on the road back to a life that I was born to step into.

I remember my first three goals like it was yesterday:

1. Find a 20-hour-a-week, part-time job that allowed me to work from home so I could spend time on my personal business and dreams.
2. Publicly launch my own business, The BEAM Life, so that I could impact women all over the world to see and know their worth.
3. Implement a daily gratitude practice so that I could find peace in the present and reduce the resentment that divorce can bring.

Each of those goals had phases and things that had to be executed like building a resume, applying for jobs, leaning into my network, applying for an LLC, refining a morning routine, etc.

Having the world and my life turned upside down was hard, and without having these foundations of goal-setting, I would've most likely continued to stay in a state of panic and victim mentality. Instead, I felt complete clarity and found a way forward.

And through it all, I knew that I needed to share this powerful strategy with you, too!

My hope for you is that over these last 90 days, you've seen a side of yourself that has been hiding for a really long time. I hope you found that inner confidence, that strong, resilient, and fearless woman who is deserving of living her Happily Ever Now!

If I'm being honest, I'm terrible with endings—so instead, I want you to think of this as just the beginning of our relationship. In fact, I have a special gift for you as a congratulations for choosing to *Be Everything And More*.

Head on over to the Facebook Group, and share your biggest takeaway from this 90-day goal-setting experience. Tag me, and I'll give you lifetime access to my three-day Level Up Your Life Bootcamp, where I breakdown limiting beliefs, boundary setting, stress management, and prioritizing your current commitments.

Can't wait to see what's waiting for you on the other side!

xx

-Coach Kaitlin

www.ingramcontent.com/pod-product-compliance
Lightning Source LLC
Chambersburg PA
CBHW060918120626
46553CB00001B/369